"Before I formed
you in the womb I knew you…"
Jeremiah 1:5 (NIV)

Come and know Me.

Know Me

A Daily Devotional
for Women

KNOW ME

ISBN 978-1-7373032-3-7

Published by:
Palau Publishing
PO Box 50
Portland, Oregon 97207

Cover design and layout: Katie Bredemeier
Cover painting and art direction: Wendy Palau

Printed in England
24 25 26 27 // PP // 5 4 3 2 1

Know Me

A Daily Devotional
for Women

BY WENDY PALAU

with Eva Beckwith and Charlotte Sanchez

TABLE OF
Contents

Introduction

from Wendy Palau

I wrote this devotional specifically with you in mind. My sister, I don't know your full story. I don't know what you have been through. Where you're coming from. What pain you have endured. What joys you have experienced. But there is One who does know. And His name is Jesus.

My friend, whatever your story has been to this point, I can promise you this: God has so much more in store for you. He is a loving, generous, forgiving, all-knowing, grace-filled Father. And He wants nothing but the best for you.

Your life is a journey. I pray you know that. Where you are today— it is not the end. In many ways, it is just the beginning. And God wants to shower you with His love and goodness.

Take heart! Whether your life has been full of joy or heartache, God is leading you into a life full of overwhelming joy one step at a time. It is a spiritual journey.

And it definitely will be an adventure!

Like any good adventure, there will be ups and downs, good days and bad days. From my experience, there's only one authentic way to move forward on your spiritual journey with God—only one way to avoid getting stuck or lost…

That secret is to meet with God every day. Connect with Him. Talk to Him. Share your concerns and fears. And listen to Him speak hope and wisdom and comfort and direction to you.

"But how?" you may ask. "How do you hear from God? I've asked. I've pleaded. But I never hear His voice."

God speaks primarily through His Word, the Bible. It's His inspired words to us. But He also speaks through friends, through His Spirit, through that "still small voice," as the Bible calls it. And if you take the time to quiet your heart and listen for His voice, you will hear Him.

There are beautiful words from the Bible in the book of **Psalms, chapter 25**. The writer is asking God for this very thing...

> *Show me how you work, GOD;*
> *School me in your ways.*
> *Take me by the hand;*
> *Lead me down the path of truth.*
> *You are my Savior, aren't you?*
> *—Psalm 25:4-5 (MSG)*

What a beautiful prayer! So honest. So real. There have been many times in my life when I could relate to this exact prayer.

As we walk through the world, we need to understand how God works. We are constantly bombarded with lies, but the God of all truth is ready and waiting to reveal His perfect wisdom and insight to us. As we learn His ways, we are changed, we are encouraged, and the truth shines brighter than the lies.

God, through His son Jesus, has made a way for us to have a relationship with Him. And He's given us His very self—in the form of His Holy Spirit—who promises to be an advocate, counselor, and friend.

That's what this book is about, my friend. Helping you, through the words and wisdom of the Bible, to hear the voice of the Holy Spirit speaking directly to you, directly into your life and your circumstances.

Listen to His heart. He calls you daughter. He sees you. He knows you. He loves you. He is with you—right now. He calls to you with a calm and compassionate voice, *"Come to me, my daughter. Let me carry your burdens. I will never leave you.*

I will never let you down. I am offering you hope today. Will you receive it?"

As you read this book, as you pore over God's words, His love and truth for you, know that I am praying for you. I know what it's like to feel alone and in despair. But the God of the universe is here for you. He is with you. And that changes everything!

"This hope is a strong and trustworthy anchor for our souls. It leads us through the curtain into God's inner sanctuary. Jesus has already gone in there for us. He has become our eternal High Priest..." — Hebrews 6:19-20 (NLT)

How To Use This Book

This book is intended to be used in your daily devotional times to help you know God more deeply and personally. Be still and know He is with you as you read one page each day. Every page focuses on one simple yet profound thought to help you understand Him more clearly, and offers a prayer to help you draw closer to Him.

You will find this book is divided into seven categories, each one beginning with a story about Jesus' interaction with a real live woman in the Bible.

Although you can find each one of these stories in the Bible, in this book they are written from the perspective of the women— what they may have been thinking or feeling, encountering Jesus in real time. Read these as you would read poetry. They are not intended to be treated as what actually took place. There is no way to know for sure what was going on in the hearts and minds of these women.

Place yourself in the story and imagine how it would feel to receive the care, compassion, love, and dignity with which Jesus treated these women.

God wants nothing less for you. To read the full Bible stories of these amazing encounters, go to the scripture passages listed at the bottom of each page.

By the time you finish this book, I believe you will know God's love, forgiveness, rest, care, compassion, and presence in a whole new way. He is with you, even now.

Know Me—
I Know
and
Love You

Jesus and the
Woman at the Well

"Come and see a man who told me everything I ever did!
Could he possibly be the Messiah?"—John 4:29 (NLT)

In the heat of midday, I come to draw water from the same old well…
A normal chore. A normal day.
But today, a man is waiting—tired and thirsty.
He asks me for a drink.
But *this—this* is not normal.
This kind of man does not talk to a woman like me.
A lowly woman. An outcast woman.
Sir, you have no bucket. You have no rope.
Why do you ask me for a drink?
He says God has a gift for me.
He says it's living water…that I will never thirst again.
And then—that unimaginable moment.
He tells me He knows me.
He lists my sins. He knows my fears. He sees just how thirsty I am.
But in His eyes, there's only kindness.
In His presence, I feel a dignity I've never known.
And I know…
He is not just a man but the Savior of the world.
Offering water from an eternal well.
Life that never runs out.

Jesus says to you, today, "I know you. Come know Me."

God, You know me completely. I want to know You more.
Take me on a journey of closeness with You. Amen.

Read the full Bible story in John 4:1-30.

Friend:
one attached to another by affection

There is no greater love than to lay down one's life for one's friends. —John 15:13 (NLT)

Our world is a lonely place. Though we long for connection, good friends are hard to find. And even with the best of friends, our souls long for a deeper kind of connection than any human can provide.

Bring all your loneliness and come know the Friend who loves you like no other.

He knows you better than you know yourself. He wants to be with you—even closer than a brother or sister.

He has laid down His life for you!

He calls you "friend," and longs to be with you. Spend time with Him today.

Come to Him with all your needs. He will not abandon you.

I am lonely, Lord. You know. Please come.
Help me. I need Your friendship. Thank You for
laying down Your life for me. Amen.

Familiar:

closely and intimately acquainted

**You made all the delicate, inner parts of my body
and knit me together in my mother's womb.** —*Psalm 139:13* (NLT)

Jesus knows you.

He created you. He knows every thought you have—everything you've ever done or will do.

Imagine…He formed you out of nothing before your first breath. What a beautiful image. He is the loving Creator of all things—including us.

This shouldn't scare you. This should comfort you.

Jesus knows your battles, your struggles, your past, and your future.

Jesus knows what you've done, and He knows what has been done to you.

Jesus is familiar with you, and He loves you.

Do you believe this?

You can entrust your life to Him. He is the Father who loves you. And He's waiting for you to come home.

Today is your day. Return to the loving arms of the One who knows you—Jesus.

---

*God, everything I have tried to hide…I bring it to You. You see
and know me deeply. You misunderstand nothing about me.
Take care of me. I put my life in Your hands. Amen.*

Wanted:

wished for, desired, intended

***Afterward Jesus went up on a mountain
and called out the ones he wanted to go with him.
And they came to him.
—Mark 3:13 (NLT)***

When Jesus called His first followers, these were the people that He wanted to be with Him. People who would walk with Him. They were regular people. Not well-educated, not famous, not wealthy. Just regular people whom He wanted.

Jesus wants you.

He wants to be with you. Not just to straighten out your life. He wants a relationship with you.

When He called these friends…He called them to be with Him. He wants the same for you.

He wants to have a friendship with you.

To be with you…
To dwell in you…
A daily, intimate friendship.

---

*God, thank You that although You made the whole universe,
You want to be with me. Lord, You don't need me—You want me,
and You have chased me down and drawn near to me. I say "yes"
to Your presence. I want to be with You. Amen.*

Companion:

one who lives with and serves another

Mary responded, "Oh, how my soul praises the Lord. How my spirit rejoices in God my Savior! For he took notice of his lowly servant girl, and from now on all generations will call me blessed. For the Mighty One is holy, and he has done great things for me."
—Luke 1:46-49 (NLT)

Life can be lonely…even with many people around. Sometimes the people we love the most die or they abandon us. You must not forget, there is an Eternal Companion.

The Mighty One has taken notice of you.

You are not alone.
God knows you and He sees you.
He says to you today, "I love you."

Jesus came to the earth and gave His life…**for you.**
One of the names of God is Emmanuel. It means, **God is with us.**
And it means **God is with you.**

Jesus, I feel so alone. You came to the world, and I know You came for me. I receive You now. Be near to me in my loneliness. Help me to feel Your closeness. Thank You for coming into this broken world and into my broken life. I give my life to You. Amen.

Love:

warm attachment, devotion, strong affection

Long ago the Lord said to Israel:
"I have loved you, my people, with an everlasting love.
With unfailing love I have drawn you to myself."
—Jeremiah 31:3 (NLT)

God loves the world, but does He love me?

We can believe that a powerful God sees the world and loves it, yet, we struggle to believe that **He sees us**…our intimate thoughts…our sins, our struggles…and He still loves us.

It's not a partial love.
Not a love with "buts."
Not a love with conditions.
It is not mixed with disapproval.
It is eternal—everlasting and perfect.

He knows us…and He loves us!

God is love. And His love toward us is not dependent on our perfection but on His perfection.

God loves you now.
He loves you completely.

God, I believe and receive Your full, boundless,
perfect love right now. In Jesus' name. Amen.

Everlasting:
continuing, enduring through all time

Give thanks to the Lord, for he is good!
His faithful love endures forever.
—Psalm 107:1 (NLT)

Love is the most overused and abused word. We say *"I love my dog, I love ice cream, I love my new shoes, and I love my children"* —all using the same word!

Do I feel the same affection toward all of these things? No! There's a love that means I really like something or a love that means I would do anything for this person…even die.

God's love is free of human frailties…our confusing emotions…our tainted affections.

God says, "I love you," and He means it.

He likes you.
He wants to spend time with you.
He understands everything about you.

He would do anything for you—even die. And, He did!

God, thank You that Your love for me is pure, unchangeable, and unlimited. Help me to remember You do not love the way humans do. Your love is deeper, wider, and stronger than I can even imagine. Help me understand Your amazing love. I receive it today. Amen.

Treasure:
something of great worth or value

**And I will give you treasures hidden in the darkness—
secret riches. I will do this so you may know that I am the L**ORD**,
the God of Israel, the one who calls you by name.
—Isaiah 45:3 (**NLT**)**

God has treasure for you—precious things that cannot be taken away.

Diamonds originate deep inside the earth, in the base of the thickest, oldest, and darkest parts of the continents. Pressure is what creates diamonds. Lots and lots of pressure in the depths of the earth.

It's the same with us, in our lives.

God has treasures for you—things you can only learn through pressure. He calls them the treasures of darkness.

The way God shows up for you in your time of deepest need. The way He cares for you when you are feeling the most afraid, grief-stricken, and vulnerable. It's here we find great treasure…the treasure is Him. His presence in the darkest moments of life.

In that place of reliance on Him, you realize the beauty, the treasure of God—He is who He says He is. He is as good as He promised. And He will never leave you.

Lord, I thank You for Your constant faithfulness. In the darkest moments of my life, You are with me. Even right now. I pray and believe that You will bring treasures from the darkness. Precious revelations of Your trustworthy and steadfast love—for me. Amen.

Trust:
to be sure, secure, to hide for refuge

Fearing people is a dangerous trap,
but trusting the LORD means safety.
—Proverbs 29:25 *(NLT)*

People have opinions.

These opinions are launched off into the world so easily, quickly, and frequently. And we become confused, swayed by the noise of so many ideas. We are impacted by what other people think, and with all the conflicting voices, it can be hard to know who and what to believe.

Only one opinion should matter.

Just be quiet. Listen. It's the whisper of the Spirit of Truth, giving us hope, and reminding us of what is true.

What are you listening to? Today, turn off the noise of other people's opinions and listen instead to the words of the Father who loves you.

Father, help me to quiet my mind. Sort out every anxious thought.
Put each one to rest. I want to focus all my heart and mind on You.
Help me, Lord, to trust Your opinion above all others. Amen.

Perseverance:

endurance, steadfastness, patient waiting

...And let us run with endurance the race God has set before us. We do this by keeping our eyes on Jesus, the champion who initiates and perfects our faith. Because of the joy awaiting him, he endured the cross, disregarding its shame... —Hebrews 12:1b-2a (NLT)

Jesus starts + completes our faith (not on us!)

His why!

Let this comfort you...

Our journeys are bumpy roads, ups and downs, round and round. Each of us has our past habits, our weaknesses, and our scars.

We are not alone in it.
We don't have to figure it all out ourselves.

God is within you through every step. He will be faithful to finish what He started in you. He is the author of your story and the redeemer of every detail.

He has done all that is needed for you to continue walking along the path He has for you.

Persevere today.

Lord, my life, my story is in Your hands. I trust You to carry me. I trust You to finish what You started. You are perfecting my faith and moving me toward Your perfect plan. Amen.

Know My Forgiveness

Jesus and the Woman Caught in Adultery

Then Jesus stood up again and said to the woman, "Where are your accusers? Didn't even one of them condemn you?" —John 8:10 (NLT)

I am dragged from the shadows. The morning light stings. I am taken.
    I am shoved. I am exposed. But he slinks away.
Rough hands drag me, threatening violence.
Behind their force, there is a plan. They thrust my body toward the One
    who's teaching. Hundreds of eyes burn into me.
Teacher! Teacher! This woman was caught in adultery! the rough men sneer.
The law says to stone her to death. What do you say?
Down to the ground the teacher stoops. Still silent as they press Him, He
    writes in the dust with His finger.
Roaring, they demand an answer.
Unshaken still, the Teacher speaks…
Let the one who has never sinned throw the first stone.
I brace for pain and hope for the end to come quickly.
And the Teacher stoops again to write in the dust.
One by one, those angry men slip away. First, the oldest. Until only the
    Teacher remains. He stands beside me.
Where are your accusers? Didn't even one of them condemn you?
No, Lord.
Neither do I. Go and sin no more.

The religious leaders came to test—Jesus came to teach.
They came to humiliate—Jesus came to honor.
They came angry at her—they left angry at Him.
They defined this woman by her past—Jesus defined her by her future.

Lord, thank You for standing between me and my accusers.
Only You can make me free. Amen.

Read the full Bible story in John 8:1-11.

Mercy:
compassionate treatment of those in distress

**People who conceal their sins will not prosper,
but if they confess and turn from them, they will receive mercy.
—Proverbs 28:13 (NLT)**

We all have secrets. Things from the past that haunt us. Struggles
we wrestle with silently.

But you can't hide from God. He knows everything you do and
everything you think. Don't run and hide. Instead, be comforted.

He knows it all, and He still loves you.

There is a way forward. Your sin, your failures, and your internal
struggles do not determine your future. God's forgiveness does.

Confess everything to God.

Come before the Lord without fear and don't conceal your failures
from Him. Turn onto a new path. Humble yourself before Him.
He is merciful and kind.

He will forgive you. Jesus purchased this forgiveness and freedom
with His very own body. It is for you.

Receive it.

---

*Lord, I have done wrong. I am turning from sin today. Remove it from
my life. Thank You, Jesus, for giving me freedom. Amen.*

Receive:

to begin to contain or possess

**He has removed our sins as far from us
as the east is from the west.
—Psalm 103:12 (NLT)**

We can doubt God's forgiveness.

We wonder, "Does He remember the wrong things I've done? The things that have damaged my life and hurt others?"

We all have regrets.

There are mistakes that we agonize over. They torment us. We long to go back and choose differently. But we can't change the past.

Today, I want to convince you of what is true.

Jesus went to the cross for you. On that day, He covered the sins of your past, your present, and your future.

The enemy of our souls wants you to believe that God remembers your failures—that He is disappointed in you. This is a lie.

Because of Jesus, your sin is gone. It is finished. Jesus has removed it, once and for all.

Receive His forgiveness.

---

*Jesus, Your sacrifice was more than enough to pay for my sins.
I let go of regret. I rest in the security of Your forgiveness. Amen.*

Human:

one who feels human emotions and vulnerabilities

***...rather, he [Jesus] made himself nothing by taking the
very nature of a servant, being made in human likeness.
—Philippians 2:7 (NIV)***

God became human.

The ultimate deity became a human. What a mystery!

The most powerful One loves humanity.

He loves us enough to put aside His mighty power and become one of
us. He experienced everything it means to be human. The heartache,
the joy, the humiliation, the weariness.

Because...
He cares about people. He cares about you.

He was not content to be separated from us. So He became like us,
and He willingly died for us.

Let this truth awaken awe, gratitude, and humility within you today.

---

*Lord, You are so good. I meditate on Your glory...the ultimate deity.
I consider how You humbled Yourself, becoming human. I am
overwhelmed by Your love. Thank You for becoming one of us. Amen.*

Paradox:
a seemingly contradictory statement or quality

God has spoken plainly, and I have heard it many times:
Power, O God, belongs to you; unfailing love, O Lord, is yours.
—Psalm 62:11-12a (NLT)

We often misunderstand God. Our life experiences cause us to develop warped ideas of what God is really like.

We lean in one direction or the other—

Maybe we think God is soft, jolly, happy, and just wants to please us.

Maybe we think God is hard—a stern father, sitting back with His arms folded…waiting for us to fail.

Here is the truth: God is the perfect balance of both love and power.

He cares for us with tender love. He guides and provides for us with His power.

God is not who we imagined Him to be. He is who He is. And He is good!

God, I trust Your love—that You will care for me tenderly.
Draw me close. I trust Your strength to guide me, lead me,
and help me when I am weak. Amen.

Jealous:

demanding faithfulness and exclusive worship

***You must not bow down to them or worship them, for I,
the Lord your God, am a jealous God who will not tolerate
your affection for any other gods...***
—Exodus 20:5a (NLT)

We know that selfish jealousy is wrong and destructive. It says,
"You have something I want, and I'm angry I can't have it."

But God's holy jealousy comes from a beautiful place of love.

The God of the universe loves you so much that He feels jealousy
when your affections turn elsewhere.

He wants your deepest love because He has the deepest love for you.

He wants to occupy the very center of your heart.

He knows how we injure our souls when our hearts drift from Him.

Center your love on Him, and let Him be your focus.

God's jealousy is care, concern, and protectiveness.

Let it draw you closer to Him.

---

*Lord, I love You with my whole heart. You are the
center of my life. I give You all the glory and honor.
You are worthy of all my love. Amen.*

Redeem:

to free from captivity by payment of ransom

Praise the Lord, my soul, and forget not all his benefits—who forgives all your sins and heals all your diseases, who redeems your life from the pit and crowns you with love and compassion…
—Psalm 103:2-4 (NLT)

Imagine yourself in a pit.

A dark, deep place. You're trapped, alone, and dirty.
You want to escape.

God has redeemed you from a life that is like a pit. He rescued you. He pulled you out. He set you free and made you clean.

Jesus came to redeem us.

The word redeem means to set us free by purchasing our freedom. This is exactly what Jesus did on the cross. He offered up His life for yours.

He went down to the pit so you could be lifted out.

Lord, You know my life. You know where I have been, and You know where I want to be…with You. God, I am stuck. Come with Your redeeming power. Rescue me. Amen.

Waiting:
remaining in readiness and expectation

Praise the Lord, the God of Israel, because he has visited and redeemed his people. He has sent us a mighty Savior from the royal line of his servant David, just as he promised through his holy prophets long ago. —Luke 1:68-70 (NLT)

Waiting is hard. We wait for circumstances to change. We wait for a chance to rest from our work. We wait to be with the people we love.

Maybe you have been waiting.

Maybe you know you need help.

Before Jesus was born, God's people had been waiting, anticipating the arrival of a Savior—the promised Messiah who would come to take away the sins of the world. To draw people back to the Lord. They waited and longed for Him.

And Jesus came.

He came for the entire world...and He came for you.

His birth all those years ago—was for you. His coming is personal.

Ask Jesus to come closer. Invite Him into every area of your life. Hold nothing back from Him.

Thank You, Jesus, for coming...for me. Have every part of my life. I hold nothing back. I want to honor You, follow You, worship You, and love You with all that is within me. My life is Yours. Amen.

Eternity:

a seemingly endless or immeasurable time

I give them eternal life, and they will never perish. No one can snatch them away from me, for my Father has given them to me, and he is more powerful than anyone else. No one can snatch them from the Father's hand. —*John 10:28-29* (NLT)

Your house will not last forever. Your possessions will not last forever.

People are the one thing that lasts. We are eternal souls.

We will live forever. God offers us the privilege of spending eternity with Him, free from death and separation.

This beautiful gift is free to us, but costly to Him.

God gave His only Son, Jesus—sacrificed so we could be with Him.

Your salvation in Jesus Christ is a promise you can count on. Jesus chose to give Himself for you. Your eternity is secure in Him.

Jesus, everything around me will fade. Help me to focus on what will last…Your promises and the people You love. Amen.

Exchange:
the act of giving or taking one thing in return for another

My old self has been crucified with Christ. It is no longer I who live, but Christ lives in me. So I live in this earthly body by trusting in the Son of God, who loved me and gave himself for me.
—Galatians 2:20 (NLT)

This is the great exchange:

You let your old self die and start a new life through Christ. You let your old desires pass away and become filled with the Holy Spirit and His desires.

Life from death. This is what the cross is all about. When you submit your life to Him, His Spirit comes and lives in you.

The powerful presence of God—His very life—comes to fill you.

Be filled with His deep joy and peace. Be filled with His presence. Be filled with His hope.

You don't lose your personality when you become new in Christ. You gain a new abundance that takes you beyond yourself. You'll come to love what God loves and want what He wants.

Lord, I give You my life.
Take my old ways and give me a new start in You, Jesus. Amen.

Know My Rest

Jesus and Martha of Bethany

There is only one thing worth being concerned about. Mary has discovered it, and it will not be taken away from her. —Luke 10:42 (NLT)

I see the dust hover in the distance.
The Teacher is on His way.
Lord, let me be worthy of His visit!
Teacher, come in here! Let me feed You. I have what You need.
From the kitchen, I hear the lilt of relaxed conversation.
The warm timbre of the Teacher's voice, but can't make out His words.
My sister's laughter sings out amidst the voices of our honored guests.
I need to hear His wisdom.
Instead, I wipe sweat from my brow.
Frustration boils. I cannot keep it in.
Lord, doesn't it seem unfair to You that my sister just sits here while I do all the work? Tell her to come and help me.
Surely, He will correct her—my foolish and inconsiderate sister.
But He surprises me…
My dear Martha, you are worried and upset over all these details. There is only one thing worth being concerned about. Mary has discovered it, and it will not be taken away from her.

He loves you. You have nothing to prove. Nothing to earn.
Come into His rest.

God, You are the only One who gives real rest. Settle me down with Your love. I want to be still in Your presence. Amen.

Read the full Bible story in Luke 10:38-42.

Peace:

freedom from hostility; complete tranquility

And just as they were telling about it, Jesus himself was suddenly standing there among them. "Peace be with you," he said.
—Luke 24:36 (NLT)

"Peace be with you." These were the first words Jesus said to His disciples after His resurrection from the dead.

Peace—one thing every human needs.

We sing, talk, and protest for it…we even fight for it. We need peace in our lives and homes. We need peace in our minds and souls. The world is desperate for peace.

Peace means wholeness…to join or tie together…our greatest need, met. When Jesus overcame death, the hostility and separation between God and all people was immediately dealt with.

God made a way for us to be at peace with Him and at peace with others.

He says to you today, **"Peace be with you."** Receive this gift.

Lord, I am desperate for peace.
Thank You for offering it to me. I receive Your peace,
Your wholeness, and Your presence. Amen.

Tend:

to apply one's self to the care of; to watch over

**Still other seeds fell on fertile soil, and they produced a crop
that was thirty, sixty, and even a hundred times as much as
had been planted! —Matthew 13:8 (NLT)**

We make ourselves so busy. Always working and striving to become better, stronger, efficient, and productive.

Striving can be an obsession…a burden.

We feel if we can just move faster, we will win at life.

What we really need is to let Jesus tend to us.

A seed planted in the ground needs water, air, and sunlight. With these needs met, it grows. It produces. It feels miraculous.

Jesus tells of a gardener who scattered seeds. Some sprouted and withered in bad soil. But when we walk with Him—when we know Him—we become rooted in the good soil of Jesus.

He will grow you and change you from the inside out.
Allow Him to tend to your soul.

---

*Lord, I don't want to spend my life scrambling to cross
an imaginary finish line. Tend me as a seed in Your garden.
Root me in Your good soil. Nourish my spirit. Amen.*

Release:

set free from confinement, burden, or oppression

Seek the Kingdom of God above all else, and live righteously, and he will give you everything you need. So don't worry about tomorrow, for tomorrow will bring its own worries. Today's trouble is enough for today. —Matthew 6:33-34 (NLT)

As much as you wish it weren't true, you often find yourself worrying.

We worry about time, our children, and money. Sometimes we worry about every little thing. At times, it feels impossible not to worry. Worry leads to anxiety.

We can have victory over this constant cycle.

Remember…believe…God knows what you need.

He knows all that is happening in your life, down to the tiniest detail. *He knows, He cares, and He will guide you through it.*

When worries overtake you…

Focus only on God. Believe He will take care of you.

Release the worry.

Lord, I trust You.
I release my worry, anxiety, and every anxious thought.
I give You my full attention. Amen.

Carry:
to bear the weight or burden of something

**So humble yourselves under the mighty power of God,
and at the right time he will lift you up in honor. Give all your
worries and cares to God, for he cares about you.
—1 Peter 5:6-7 (NLT)**

Anxiety…

The word means different things to different people.

"Anxiety" means *"distress, or uneasiness of mind caused by fear or
danger or misfortune."*

This is a real thing. Everyone experiences it on some level. It arrives
with life's challenges. It can pass quickly, or come and go for years.

Anxiety can be debilitating.

**There is Someone who is bigger than your anxiety. There is One who
is stronger than your fear.**

Trust Him with all that causes you anxiety. He can carry the weight
you were never meant to carry…your worry and your fear.

Let God carry you today. He is the One who cares for you.

---

*Lord, I place every anxious thought in Your powerful
and loving hands. Help me. Quiet my fears and ease my struggle.
I know You will care for me. Amen.*

Promise:

a binding declaration that one will do something specific

I am leaving you with a gift—peace of mind and heart.
And the peace I give is a gift the world cannot give.
So don't be troubled or afraid. —John 14:27 (NLT)

Jesus said, ***"I do not give to you as the world gives."***

We frustrate ourselves striving for peace. Many convincing voices tell us what we should do to find it. Most are empty promises offering fulfillment that never comes.

God's promises are sure.

He is faithful and trustworthy. He keeps His word. The peace He offers is different from the peace the world promises.

God offers something so much better. He offers Himself!

He, Himself is our peace. Press deep into knowing Jesus. His peace will find you. There is no frustrating search needed. Invest in an intimate relationship with Him.

Jesus' gift of peace is waiting for you.

Lord, I don't want to search the world for temporary ways to find peace.
I want to find deep and unshakeable peace in You.
Help me to know You more. Amen.

Truth:

the category of real things, events, and facts

**The LORD is my light and my salvation—so why should I be afraid?
The LORD is my fortress, protecting me from danger,
so why should I tremble? —Psalm 27:1 (NLT)**

Anxious thoughts can arrive like unwelcome guests.

Anxiety is...fear that won't leave you alone. Unfounded, crippling fear has one source. It comes from the father of lies, the enemy of our souls. Anxious thoughts that have no basis in logic are nothing more than lies.

You don't have to listen to these lies.

Call the lies what they are. Realize that they are an attack designed to steal your peace and joy. Call on the God of peace.

Tell fear and anxiety to leave you alone. Reject the lies, and tell yourself what is true.

The truth is, peace is your inheritance in Christ Jesus. The work Jesus did on the cross—His power over death and the grave—has brought security and peace to all humanity.

The peace of Christ belongs to you.

---

*God, because You are mighty and powerful,
and because You love me, I have nothing to fear.
Will you come and fill me with Your peace right now? Amen.*

Beloved:
a person who is held close to the heart

**Such love has no fear, because perfect love expels all fear.
If we are afraid, it is for fear of punishment, and this shows
that we have not fully experienced his perfect love.
—1 John 4:18 (NLT)**

If we let it, fear can rule us. It is powerful. Living in fear is debilitating.

It will shrink our lives and isolate us. It will kill our relationships. It will prevent us from taking healthy risks.

The enemy of our souls loves to play on our fears.

Jesus offers us something better. He calls us His beloved children.

His Holy Spirit draws us close. He fills us with His love—the opposite of fear. He offers a beautiful life of love, faith, and hope.

Love overrules fear.

Know you are loved by almighty God. Let your fear melt away.

---

*Lord, I come to You with all my fear. I pray You would take it and instead
give me faith in Your great love. You are not a punishing, cruel God.
You are a giver, and I put my trust in You. Amen.*

Reign:
to have sovereign power

For a child is born to us, a son is given to us. The government will rest on his shoulders. And he will be called: Wonderful Counselor, Mighty God, Everlasting Father, Prince of Peace.
—Isaiah 9:6 (NLT)

Wonderful Counselor. Mighty God. Everlasting Father. Prince of Peace.

Jesus fulfilled all these powerful titles.

He is our Prince of Peace.

His peace is meant to reign over our lives like a good king. He has the authority to bestow peace.

When chaos abounds—or even when our lives are going smoothly—**we long deep inside for peace.** We cannot create it by ourselves.

It feels out of reach, even as we grasp for it.

But Jesus offers it to us. He has obtained it for us. He says, "I will be your peace. I will be the bridge between you and an Almighty God—come and let me rule over your life with My peace."

Jesus, Prince of Peace, come and flood my life. You can give me the deepest kind of peace, regardless of my circumstances. You are my peace. Amen.

Bear:

to support the weight of something

**Yet it was our weaknesses he carried; it was our sorrows
that weighed him down. And we thought his troubles were a
punishment from God, a punishment for his own sins! But he was
pierced for our rebellion, crushed for our sins. He was beaten so
we could be whole. He was whipped so we could be healed.**
—Isaiah 53:4-5 (NLT)

Jesus is the ruler with authority and dominion. Yet, He is the bearer of all our most oppressive burdens.

He chose to bear the punishment for our sins so we would not have to.

When Jesus went to the cross, He took the suffering and heaviness of sin…on behalf of the whole world…on Himself.

Jesus, the one who had never sinned, paid the price for all.

He wants us to live in the freedom He obtained for us.

Allow Him to free you from sin and shame. Allow Him to lift all your heavy burdens.

---

*God, thank You for rescuing me. Come, carry what is heavy.
Come, lift what hurts. Everything that is oppressive in my life,
I hand it over to You. Amen.*

Know My Compassion

Jesus and
Mary of Bethany

Jesus told her, "I am the resurrection and the life. Anyone who believes in me will live, even after dying." —John 11:25 (NLT)

*For four days, my vision has been blurred by tears. My own wailing
        drowning out all other sounds.
My dear brother is dead, wrapped in graveclothes in a tomb.
        Nothing they say will soothe this pain.
The One I hoped for did not come. The Healer was not here.
Disappointment overwhelms me.
My sister is at the doorway.*
Mary, the Teacher wants to see you.
I rush to fall at His feet.
Lord, if only you had been here, my brother would not have died.
His eyes reflect my pain. He asks, **Where have you put him?**
*Jesus weeps.
They whisper hushed opinions.
Look at His tender love! But why wasn't He here when it mattered?
His voice pierces the air, "Roll the stone aside!"
His prayer resounds…*
**Father, thank you for hearing me. You always hear me, but I say it out
        loud for the sake of all these people standing here so that
        they will believe you sent me.**
*Lazarus, come out!
My brother, alive, steps from the shadows.
Death evaporates. Shouts of joy shake the earth.*

*Jesus knew Mary's pain and He knows yours, too. He weeps with you.
He walks with you. He speaks life into your deepest darkness.*

*Lord, I don't want to hide my pain from You anymore.
I am home safe in Your compassion. Amen.*

Read the full Bible story in John 11:1-44.

Compassion:

empathy toward others' distress; desire to alleviate it

**The LORD is good to everyone.
He showers compassion on all his creation.
—Psalm 145:9 (NLT)**

God is not like us.

Our God is a God of compassion. For us, compassion is an emotion that comes and goes. His compassion is not like ours.

His compassion is perfect.

If all the conditions are right, we can have compassion for others. But if something is amiss, the compassion in our hearts will take a pause.

This is not the way of Jesus. He is pure, sinless, consistent compassion. Perfect care. Compassion is His constant posture toward all people:

To the rich and the poor
The powerful and the powerless
The abuser and the abused
The victimizer and the victim

And His compassion is for you, today.

---

*God, Your compassion never ends, never changes, never fails.
Thank You for being compassionate toward me.
Fill me with Your compassion. Amen.*

Relief:

removal of something oppressive, painful, or distressing

He will wipe every tear from their eyes, and there will be no more death or sorrow or crying or pain. All these things are gone forever. —Revelation 21:4 (NLT)

No more death, sorrow, crying, or pain. This is a promise of what is to come. At the end of the age, we'll see Jesus face to face. We will be with Him forever!

Imagine…suffering gone…forever!

You have cried tears…of frustration, grief, loneliness, anger, disappointment, neglect, yearning. In some miraculous way, God Himself will wipe away these tears.

Treasure this thought…all of your broken places—fully healed. What a relief it will be!

This promise is for you. And you can rejoice in it now.

Receive hope in God's great compassion—every tear wiped away.

God, I still suffer…I still have pain in my life. But I rejoice now in Your promise of relief. I know the hope that awaits me. Strengthen me until the beautiful day when You make all things right. Amen.

Constant:

marked by firm, steadfast resolution or faithfulness

**The LORD is merciful and compassionate,
slow to get angry and filled with unfailing love.
—Psalm 145:8 (NLT)**

God feels compassion toward you. He wants you to trust that His compassion is constant.

Do you believe that His posture toward you right now is compassion?

You might think, "My life is troubled right now. God seems hard and distant. His eyes have looked elsewhere."

This is not so. **That thought is a lie.**

You might think, *"I know He has compassion, but I've let Him down. My sin, my addictive ways, my pride…I'm certain He's frustrated with me."*

That also is a lie.

Jesus' life was offered up…He gave it all for you. What Jesus did on the cross can never change. And the compassion that took Him there doesn't change. It never will.

His tender care for you is constant.

---

*Lord, thank You for Your steadfast compassion.
I make mistakes, but You still love me.
I receive Your compassion right now. Amen.*

Life:

spiritual existence transcending physical death

And the last enemy to be destroyed is death. For the Scriptures say,
"God has put all things under his authority."
— 1 Corinthians 15:26-27 (NLT)

We don't often think about death until we're face-to-face with it.
Someone dies. We get sick. We remember that we are mortal.

Your body won't live forever.

Death comes for us all. All except one. The Creator of life is stronger
than death. He has authority over death. This is why Jesus came.

Because of His birth…
His taking of human form…
His entering into the world He created…
Because of His death…
His sacrifice to pay for our sins…
Because of His resurrection, which proved His power over death…

You can have eternal life. Life that is truly life!

Let this truth fill you with hope.

The last enemy to be defeated is death, and Jesus has destroyed it.

God, You rose from the dead, so we will rise up to be with
You when these bodies wear out. You made a way for us to live
in Your glorious presence forever! Amen.

Sacrifice:

destruction of something precious for the sake of another

But you, O Lord, are a God of compassion and mercy,
slow to get angry and filled with unfailing love and faithfulness.
—Psalm 86:15 (NLT)

The emotion most frequently attributed to Jesus is compassion. Over and over again, Jesus saw people, and He had compassion for them.

When we are moved with compassion, we act. Jesus acted to relieve the suffering of the people He encountered.

God feels compassion toward you right now. He will act to relieve your suffering.

And He has acted. He acted with compassion when He sacrificed Himself for you. In Jesus, God has acted to restore you to Himself, the Giver of life and peace.

He sacrificed Himself on the cross so that one day you will truly be free of all suffering.

Lord, though we haven't fully tasted freedom from suffering,
we receive Your compassion. We believe in Your promise of a better day.
We are so grateful for Your sacrifice. Amen.

Hope:

desire accompanied by expectation of fulfillment

So you see, just as death came into the world through a man, now the resurrection from the dead has begun through another man.
—1 Corinthians 15:21 (NLT)

Why do death and pain feel terribly wrong?

We were created for life. We were created for growth, thriving, and overflowing joy.

The pain of this world wreaks havoc on us. But God provided hope.

Jesus came, and He died on that cross. He took the sin and the pain of this world on Himself. He overcame the one thing no human being can control—death.

He was put to death in the body, but made alive by the Spirit.

This is your hope.

One day when your body dies, you will be raised up to a new, heavenly body.

You have the greatest hope in Jesus. Without Him, there would be no hope at all.

God, meet me in the hardest places of my life. Speak hope to my heart so that the sorrow will not last forever. Because of You, a better day is coming. Amen.

Crown:
a reward of victory or mark of honor

***...who redeems your life from the pit and crowns you with love and compassion... —Psalm 103:4** (NIV)*

In ancient days, a crown was worn only by royalty with wealth and position.

God offers you an everlasting crown.

He offers an eternal position as a loved person.
You're valued and treasured.
You were beautifully made in His image.
You're a child of the King of kings.

He also offers us a crown of compassion. He sees you not with pity, but with a sense of leaning toward you.

He wants to help you, encourage you, heal you, strengthen you.

His love for you is eternal and unchanging.

His compassion for you is an everlasting crown.

---

*God, come with Your presence. Help me understand
Your great compassion. Your love for me is deeper and stronger
than I can comprehend. I receive this crown. Amen.*

Authority:

power to influence or command thought or behavior

Jesus came and told his disciples, "I have been given all authority in heaven and on earth." —Matthew 28:18 *(NLT)*

There are many voices in this world claiming to have authority. It can be confusing.

There is one voice we can count on. Jesus is the voice of true authority.

Let the confusion settle. Let the chaos of conflicting messages quiet down, and turn to Jesus.

Look to the Word of God, and pray. Ask God what to do.

He is the final authority, and He has given you the Bible as a guide. This is how you will come to know Him better. This is how you will learn what is true.

Let His authority guide you.

Lord, bring clarity to every part of my life. Silence the confusion. Speak clearly to me through Your word, and by Your Spirit. I am listening, Jesus. Amen.

Prayer:
a petition or conversation with God in word or thought

**When he saw the crowds, he had compassion on them,
because they were harassed and helpless, like sheep without a
shepherd. Then he said to his disciples, "The harvest is plentiful but
the workers are few. Ask the Lord of the harvest, therefore,
to send out workers into his harvest field."
—Matthew 9:36-38 (NIV)**

Compassion leads us to pray.

**When we are suffering, or someone we care about is suffering,
especially in impossible situations, we pray.**

We look to God. We cry out to Him. We beg Him to intervene—
to do what only He can do.

Consider a situation in your life, or the life of someone you love.
There is a difficult situation…and it's prompting compassion in you.

Respond to that compassion with prayer.

Ask the One with perfect compassion to intervene. Ask Him to help,
to rescue, to transform. He will hear and respond to your prayer.

---

*God, I lift up the person or situation that is on my heart today.
You know just what to do. You are the One with power to bring change.
Come, God, and help. Amen.*

Know My Care

Jesus and
the Widow

Father to the fatherless, defender of widows—
this is God, whose dwelling is holy. —Psalm 68:5 (NLT)

With each step, I feel my world disappear.
My only son's body…carried toward the tomb.
The dirt will swallow him up like it swallowed my husband.
I will never again see laughter in his eyes.
Never again feel his hand in mine.
Never again rest in his steady care.
Nothing can stop this well of tears.
But I hear a stranger gently say,
Don't cry…
I am too dizzy with confusion to reply.
Too bewildered to resist His approach.
He speaks to the lifeless body, as though my son can hear.
Young man, I tell you, get up!
And, oh! My boy!
Color flushes his cheeks. He sits up.
I hear my son's voice.
Hope floods my chest like oxygen.
Who is this holy Stranger who gave me back my son?

The same One who saw this grieving widow sees you. He has
compassion on you. He draws close, changes our reality, and
offers life from death.

Lord, I have never known kindness like Yours. You never abandon me.
Come close and help me. I long to feel Your care. Amen.

Read the full Bible story in Luke 7:11-17.

Shepherd:

one who guides, or a guard who tends sheep

***I am the good shepherd; I know my own sheep, and they know me,
just as my Father knows me and I know the Father. So I sacrifice
my life for the sheep.** —John 10:14-15 (NLT)*

Jesus calls Himself "The Good Shepherd."

He lays down His life for His sheep. The ultimate act of care.

Let this imagery change the way you understand Jesus. He is the One
who leads you to water for your soul. He is the One who guards you
from harm. He is the One who finds you and brings you home.

Jesus is calling you by name.
He has laid down His life for you.
Call to Him.

"Yes, I want to be loved and cared for by the Good Shepherd."

He will never leave you.
He will never hurt you.
He loves you.

"Yes, Lord. Here I am. Here is my life."

---

*Lord, You carry me and tend my wounds.
I trust You with my whole life.
Come care for me, Jesus. Amen.*

Care:

painstaking or watchful attention

**And I am certain that God, who began the good work within you,
will continue his work until it is finally finished on the day when
Christ Jesus returns. —Philippians 1:6 (NLT)**

God can change you.

Even in areas of your life that are frustrating. He can break the
patterns you long to see change. He can ease the struggles that
seem to control you.

When we are in need of Living Water, we wither. When we're
watered by true life, we flourish, turning our faces toward the light
of the world.

God is a gardener.

He is an attentive, patient, skilled gardener. Allow the gardener of your
soul to care for you. What He has started in your story, He will finish.

He is able and He is capable.

---

*Lord, I am asking You right now to come and tend to me. You are the one
who knows how to care for me. God, would you enter into the frustrating
patterns of my life, and bring healing and change? Amen.*

Belong:

to be attached or bound by birth, loyalty, or dependence

For our earthly fathers disciplined us for a few years, doing the best they knew how. But God's discipline is always good for us, so that we might share in his holiness. —Hebrews 12:10 (NLT)

Because we are human, we have problems. We bring all our flaws into our relationships, our homes, and the lives around us.

Pain and wounding from our family can deeply impact our lives. Healing may feel impossible. The hopeful truth is...

Your past is not the end of your story.

God wants to adopt you into His family. This is where you belong more than anywhere else. He is the perfect parent. You will not have a perfect life. But, you can walk daily with a perfect Father.

He'll never abuse you.
He will never leave you.
He will discipline you.
And when He does, it will be because He loves you.

---

*Lord, You are a father like no other. I welcome Your guidance.
I belong in Your care. I welcome Your discipline.
My life is secure in Your loving hands. Amen.*

Sustain:

to give support or relief; to supply with nourishment

**Give your burdens to the Lord, and he will take care of you.
He will not permit the godly to slip and fall.
—Psalm 55:22 (NLT)**

You likely have work to be done. Tasks nagging at the back of your mind. Something burdening, overwhelming, or irritating you.

Instead of letting your worries rattle around in your mind…
Instead of trying to solve an unsolvable problem right now…
Instead of allowing fear to creep in and anxiety to take hold…

Pile your troubles on His shoulders!

God is big enough and strong enough to carry your load. He is able to help you and to calm your fear. He wants to relieve you of your burdens.

Carrying these things yourself is not sustainable.
But if you let God carry them, He will sustain you.

Turn your heart to Him right now—wherever you are. Hand over your thoughts, your worries, your pain, your unfinished work.

Give your troubles to Him.

---

*Lord, here are my burdens…all the heavy things in my life.
I lay them on You, Jesus. You are the one who can properly carry them.
I know You will not let these things crush me. Amen.*

Accepted:

regarded with favor

Be merciful to me, O Lord, for I am calling on you constantly.
Give me happiness, O Lord, for I give myself to you. O Lord,
you are so good, so ready to forgive, so full of unfailing love for all
who ask for your help. Listen closely to my prayer,
O Lord; hear my urgent cry. I will call to you whenever
I'm in trouble, and you will answer me. —*Psalm 86:3-7 (NLT)*

We are emotional beings—passionate and full of vision one day, tired and cynical the next, irritated and frustrated the next. God isn't surprised by any of this.

He made you. He made your emotions. You don't have to hide from God.

With Him, every part of how He has made you is held and accepted.

He knows all your emotions, all that you're feeling and thinking and imagining. He loves you. And He says, "Come to me."

You can pour out every emotion to God. Take comfort in this. Allow Him to center you.

When your emotions begin to feel like too much, ask Him for help. Bring them all to Jesus.

God, I bring You every wonderful emotion and every terrible emotion. The ups and downs, the confusion and frustration. I ask that You would order my emotions, calm my heart, and meet me in the middle of my need. Amen.

Wrestle:

to engage in deep thought, consideration, or debate

**For the Spirit of God has made me,
and the breath of the Almighty** [El Shaddai] **gives me life.**
—Job 33:4 (NLT)

El Shaddai is the name for God that means, "The Almighty God"—
stronger and more powerful than anything or anyone.

We face unimaginable suffering, death, and loss, yet God remains
"The Almighty One."

In our suffering, we wrestle with God's power and might.

"If God is so powerful and mighty, how could this pain walk through
my door?"

This is difficult to understand. It doesn't make sense. It may not ever
make sense on this side of heaven. We wrestle to believe that there
can be suffering, and yet God is still powerful.

Your suffering is no reflection of God's power.

Even as you wrestle, lean into The Almighty One, El Shaddai. Let Him
show you that He is good.

---

*El Shaddai, You are mighty. As I wrestle with suffering,
help me continue to trust and honor You. I don't understand
why trouble comes, but I believe You are good. Amen.*

Father:

to care for or look after someone; act in responsibility for

But God showed his great love for us by sending
Christ to die for us while we were still sinners.
—Romans 5:8 (NLT)

We easily get confused about who God is and what He's like.

We might think of Him as a cruel puppet master, distantly controlling all the events we see on the news, disappointed in humanity.

This is false. The Bible tells us so many things that set these thoughts straight.

God loves us with perfect love.
Not love mixed with a selfish attitude.
He doesn't love us in order to be loved back.

He loves us because it's His character. It's who He is.

He has given us the freedom to choose to love Him back.

He is not a detached bully. He is a loving Father. He is calling to you.

God, You love me with perfection. You give me freedom.
I'm using that freedom to choose.
I choose to give You all my love. Amen.

Power:
ability to act or produce an effect

Search me, O God, and know my heart;
test me and know my anxious thoughts.
Point out anything in me that offends you, and lead me along
the path of everlasting life. —Psalm 139:23-24 (NLT)

Your mind is like a battlefield.

Your thoughts fight against each other. They are shadowy and difficult to sort out. At times, you may be winning the battle. Other times, thoughts are invasive and destructive. You end up feeling defeated, powerless to escape your own mind.

You are not alone. God is with you and He is powerful.

Jesus knows all the inner workings of your thoughts. He cares about how these thoughts affect you.

People around you may not understand, but Jesus does.

He is kind.
He is powerful.
He is able to help you.

Ask God to be present in your thoughts. Let the power of His Spirit lead you to a place of peace. He has the healing and new life you need.

God, I am inviting You to search my thoughts. You know me completely, Lord. You love me without reservation. Help me navigate destructive thoughts. Send me Your powerful peace. Amen.

Desire:

something longed for or hoped for

He fills my life with good things. My youth is renewed like the eagle's! —Psalm 103:5 (NLT)

Each person has core desires.

Our basic desires are to be loved, belong, and have a safe, fulfilling place in the world. We all have desires that are unique to our personality or where we come from.

Desire is a powerful motivator for every human being. But our disordered desires can destroy our lives. We often desire things that have great potential to hurt us and the people we love.

God promises something far better.

God will give you the desire for good things. And He will fulfill those desires. This is where you will find true contentment.

Bring the desires of your heart before the Lord.

God, here are my desires and longings. Will You come and be the source of my satisfaction? Wash away any disordered desires that are not from You. Amen.

Know My Love

Jesus and the Bleeding Woman

He gives power to the weak and strength to the powerless.
—Isaiah 40:29 (NLT)

My bleeding will not stop. I have nothing left for the doctors.
      They take everything and leave me just the same.
Twelve years. No relief, only pain.
Twelve years. Unclean and alone in my suffering.
I've heard stories of the Man who heals.
I've heard He does not turn from those cast out.
He is crossing the sea toward me.
I wait and I watch with empty hands.
No money. No dignity. No friendship.
I am jostled by the crowd pressing toward Him.
Pain throbs. I must not fall behind.
If I can just touch His robe, maybe…
I push through. I stretch out my hand…My fingertips touch Him.
Power surges through my body. I feel the change immediately.
He turns. **"Who touched my robe?"**
He knows. Trembling, I fall at His feet.
I tell Him…the bleeding stopped.
He calls me **Daughter.**
Precious, valuable, and loved.
The kindness in His voice embraces me.
"Your faith has made you well. Go in peace. Your suffering is over."

Jesus does not play favorites. Rejected and poor, rich and powerful…
we are all sons and daughters. Draw close to Him. Know that He
loves you in your most desperate hour.

Lord, I reach for You like this bleeding woman did.
Thank You for calling me daughter. Amen.

Read the full Bible story in Mark 5:21-34.

Helper:

one who changes things for the better; makes life bearable

"Never will I leave you. Never will I forsake you."
So we say with confidence,
"The Lord is my helper; I will not be afraid. What can mere
mortals do to me?" —Hebrews 13:5b-6 (NIV)

God is present in the darkest times of our lives.

Jesus spoke to His friends just before He went to die on the cross, and He promised He would never abandon them.

Yet, when He died, they were full of grief.

They did not yet know He was keeping His promise when He went to the cross.

He absorbed the suffering and sin of the world into Himself. And He sent His Holy Spirit, the Helper, to be with us always.

He is with you now, helping you, guiding you through each day.

No matter what you are facing, believe this promise—
He will be with you.

God, I have complete trust in You.
You will never leave me.
Nothing and no one can take Your presence from me. Amen.

Presence:

the fact of being present in one's immediate vicinity

**No, I will not abandon you as orphans—I will come to you.
Soon the world will no longer see me,
but you will see me. Since I live, you also will live.
—John 14:18-19 (NLT)**

"*Orphan*" means—fatherless, motherless, desolate, bereaved.

God understands that being alone in the world is the most helpless feeling.

But Jesus promised we will never be alone.

Maybe you have many people around you, lots of friends and family. But you still feel alone on a deep level—abandoned.

Oh, my friend, will you allow the One who made this promise draw close to you with His presence? You will never have to be alone again.

He wants to be with you. Allow yourself to feel His presence.

---

*God, come and be with me. Closer than close.
Because You are with me, I am not helpless. I am not rejected.
I am not an orphan. You are with me always. Amen.*

Unfailing:
steadfast, devoted, constant, inexhaustible

O Israel, hope in the LORD;
for with the LORD there is unfailing love.
His redemption overflows.
—Psalm 130:7 (NLT)

Unconditional love is hard to understand.

For humans, it is an impossible type of love.

We cannot fully give it. We cannot fully receive it.

Unconditional love is divine love. This is the unfailing love God has for you.

When God's love dwells in you, you will notice an increased capacity to love others. To love unselfishly. With no expectations. And unshakeable love. To love as He loves.

It feels impossible…it is a miracle…this kind of love is a promise for you.

God has unfailing, unconditional love for you.

Oh God, Your ways are higher than mine. Your love is unfailing and strong. Help me understand Your deep and devoted love for me. Help me give You all my love in return. Amen.

Strength:
capacity for exertion or endurance

---

*I pray that your hearts will be flooded with light so that you can
understand the confident hope he has given to those he called—
his holy people who are his rich and glorious inheritance.*
—Ephesians 1:18 (NLT)

Everyone feels pain and disappointment in life. We cannot escape it.

We can only choose to face it with hope, or without hope.

With hope—with Jesus—we get worn down on the outside but
become stronger on the inside.

Without hope—without the inward strengthening of the Lord—we can
become cynical, hard, and bitter.

It is never too late to move forward on your journey of hope.

Hope is found in a person—Jesus. If you are stuck, now is the time to
let Him carry you along.

You will face unexpected challenges in your life. There is no avoiding
it. Choose to let the hope of Jesus be your strength.

---

*God, fill me with the strength that comes only from You.
No matter the pain I'm going through right now,
I believe You are with me. Amen.*

Together:

with each other; for combined action

***Your unfailing love, O Lord, is as vast as the heavens;
your faithfulness reaches beyond the clouds.
—Psalm 36:5 (NLT)***

There is someone who looks forward to being with you, and loves you completely.

God loves you. He really loves you.

He loves you in an authentic, deep, raw, honest way. Only the person who knows you best can love you this way.

He knows all about you. He is your strong Advocate. And despite your shortcomings, He still wants to be together with you.

You might not have someone who loves you despite all your weaknesses on this earth. But the God of the universe—the Creator of all things—loves you and will be with you always.

---

*Thank You, God, that by Your Spirit,
You are the friend who is always with me. Amen.*

Personal:

relating to a specific individual in an intimate way

Direct your children onto the right path,
and when they are older, they will not leave it.
—*Proverbs 22:6 (NLT)*

Do you have children?

As mothers, it is so difficult to recognize our limitations in our children's spiritual lives. We can teach, train, guide, and direct our children. But each one must choose Jesus for themselves.

God has no grandchildren. He has only children.

This is also true for friends and relatives. We share the hope of Jesus, we speak the truth, we step out in faith…and we must trust the rest to the Holy Spirit.

Each individual person must step into their own personal relationship with Him, through faith.

Here is the promise: **God is always working.**

He's always calling, revealing, and drawing our children, our loved ones, our friends…to Himself.

Rest in this knowledge today.

Lord, I ask that Your Spirit would move in the lives of all those I love.
Draw them closer to Yourself. Amen.

Soul:

the animating principle; a person's total self

Praise the Lord, my soul; all my inmost being,
praise his holy name.
Praise the Lord, my soul, and forget not all his benefits—
who forgives all your sins and heals all your diseases...
—Psalm 103:1-3 (NIV)

What does your soul need today? Our bodies need food, water, and a good night's sleep.

Our souls also have needs.

The deep need of our souls is to honor God for who He is and remember what He's done for us. Our souls need truth.

He has forgiven you and restored you.
He has brought you through difficult times.
He has comforted you in pain and sorrow.
He has provided for you in ways you never imagined.

Don't forget all the Lord has done for you. It will benefit your soul to remember.

Speak to your very own soul, and say, *"Praise the Lord, O my soul. All my innermost being, praise Him."*

God, wake up my soul to praise You. You are worthy of all the love and praise of my heart. All glory and honor belong to you. Amen.

Light:
brightness that makes vision possible

---

*And you, my child, will be called a prophet of the Most High;
for you will go on before the Lord to prepare the way for him,
to give his people the knowledge of salvation through the
forgiveness of their sins, because of the tender mercy of our God,
by which the rising sun will come to us from heaven to shine on
those living in darkness and in the shadow of death, to guide our
feet into the path of peace.* —Luke 1:76-79 *(NIV)*

He will be the rising sun coming from heaven.

This is Jesus.

He came for the world and He came for you.

Imagine the sunrise…the slow infiltration of light that gradually makes
everything visible and beautiful.

There is no reason to go on living in darkness. Confess the things in
your life that are weighing you down like a blanket of darkness.

Allow the Lord of light to free you.

The rising sun, Jesus, wants to infiltrate your life with light. He
promises you will never have to walk in darkness again.

---

*Lord, I praise You and thank You for the coming of light.
You are the Light of the world. Amen.*

Ask:

make a request; call on for an answer

**You can ask for anything in my name, and I will do it, so that the
Son can bring glory to the Father. —John 14:13 (NLT)**

This is shocking.

We think, *"Lord, I can think of one hundred things I asked that You
didn't do. So, Lord, I'm not sure if I believe this."*

Very often, we read the first part of this passage in John 14:13—
I will do whatever you ask, and we forget the significance of the
second part of the verse—**in my name.**

Very often, we ask for things, but we ask in our name. We ask for
the things we want, not the things that are best for us or cause the
kingdom of God to flourish in our lives.

The second part of the passage says…
So that the Son may bring glory to the Father.

This changes everything.

**When we ask God to do something in prayer, do we submit all that
we ask to His name and for His glory?**

Don't stop asking God for what you need. But do ask with humility
and a focus on His kingdom.

---

*Lord, all I want, all I desire…I place in Your hands.
Would You act on my behalf to bring more of Your will into my life,
and increase the kingdom of God through me? Amen.*

Know Me Directly

Jesus and Hagar

"I have now seen the One who sees me."
—Genesis 16:13 (NIV)

My body is not my own.
I am ordered into Abram's bed and I obey.
Ordered to give my body in Sarai's place.
In my womb a baby grows. And in my heart, contempt. Hatred for the
      woman who made me this way.
She lashes back until I cannot take it anymore.
I flee to the deep desert.
I want to hide, but Someone finds me.
There by the wild spring, the angel of the LORD comes close.
"Hagar, Sarai's servant, where have you come from,
      and where are you going?"
I reply…
"I'm running away."
He sees me and the child inside of me.
He knows where I've come from and where I'm going.
He promises a future I cannot imagine.
He tells me, "**Return home…the Lord has heard the cry of your distress…**"
I am not alone.
Not now. Not ever.
You are the God who sees me.

*God sees you, too. He hears your cry. Nothing and no one can separate
you from His love. Come to Him directly—He's always ready to meet
with you.*

---

*Lord, thank You that I am not insignificant to You.
You are not too busy to hear me and see me. Amen.*

Read the full Bible story in Genesis 16:1-16.

Worship:
to honor or show reverence; extravagant respect, devotion

Praise the Lord. Praise the LORD, my soul.
I will praise the LORD all my life;
I will sing praise to my God as long as I live.
—Psalm 146:1-2 (NIV)

We are easily distracted…pulled in a thousand directions by a never-ending to-do list. The busyness of life always calls out for our attention.

A life spent scrambling from one thing to the next is not what we were made for.

Stop and remind yourself…

You were made to worship God. Bring Him all your affection.

The Psalmist, in the passage above, sings to his own soul. He's reminding himself…this is what I need most.

This is what you were made for.

Remember it!

Worship God because He is worthy. Worship because it's what you were made to do.

God, I give You all my love. I give You my thoughts.
I give You all my soul. I devote myself to You alone. You are worthy
of every breath of my lungs and every beat of my heart. Amen.

Affection:

a feeling of caring for someone; tender attachment

And they sang in a mighty chorus:
"Worthy is the Lamb who was slaughtered—
to receive power and riches and wisdom and strength
and honor and glory and blessing."
—Revelation 5:12 (NLT)

When you worship God, you are never worshiping by yourself.

Even if you are alone…there are others singing with you!

This is a powerful truth.

At any given time, somewhere in the world, other believers are unified with you in praising God.

Thousands upon thousands of angels are worshiping God every moment.

Sing to God, pray to Him, and love Him with your heart. You will be joining the worship that happens all the time in Heaven.

Bring your affection to Him today. Worship the Lord and know you are not singing alone.

God, I thank You that I can worship You in unity with believers
all around the world. I can worship You along with the angels.
I want to worship You all my days. Amen.

Posture:

position of the body or state of being for a special purpose

Come, let us worship and bow down.
Let us kneel before the LORD our maker,
for he is our God. We are the people he watches over,
the flock under his care.
If only you would listen to his voice today!
The LORD says, "Don't harden your hearts…"
—Psalm 95:6-8a (NLT)

God has given us so much freedom in the way we worship. He is not overly concerned about whether we sit or stand, sing or pray silently, kneel or dance.

The posture that matters to God in worship is the posture of your heart. Our hearts should bow down before Him and acknowledge:

He is God, and we are not.

Bring Him all your love today. Open your heart and let Him be close with you.

Know that He loves you back…perfectly and completely.

God, today I decide to worship You. With my thoughts, my words,
my actions, and my heart, I want to honor and adore You.
I give You my love right now. Amen.

Priest:

one authorized as a mediator between humans and God

**This hope is a strong and trustworthy anchor for our souls.
It leads us through the curtain into God's inner sanctuary.
Jesus has already gone in there for us.
He has become our eternal High Priest…
—Hebrews 6:19-20a** *(NLT)*

You don't need a priest, pastor, or any kind of spiritual leader in order to connect personally with God.

Jesus became your High Priest!

He made the ultimate sacrifice—Himself—to pay for your sins once and for all.

He made a way for you to be completely forgiven and intimately connected with God forever. There is nothing separating you and God. Jesus acted on your behalf to bring you into His presence.

No other priest is needed.

---

*Lord, You paid the cost once and for all to be close to me.
I draw near to You right now, Lord. Help me to feel the
presence of Your Spirit. Amen.*

Enter:
to go in; become a member or an active participant

***...for the sun stopped shining. And the curtain of the
temple was torn in two. Jesus called out with a loud voice,
"Father, into your hands I commit my spirit."
When he had said this, he breathed his last.***
—Luke 23:45-46 *(NIV)*

When Jesus walked the earth, there was a place in the temple where a thick curtain surrounded the "most holy place"—where the presence of God dwelled. It could only be entered by a high priest once a year.

When Jesus gave up His life…that curtain was torn in two.

Because of His sacrifice, there is now NOTHING that stands in between us and God.

You can enter into His very presence any time you pray to Him.

No special posture, no special words, no priest or pastor is needed.

Jesus brought you close to God Himself. You and God— together forever.

---

*Lord, I'll enter into Your presence just as I am.
Thank You, God, that nothing can separate
me from Your presence. Amen.*

Access:

permission to approach or communicate with a person

---

*And I will ask the Father, and he will give you another Advocate,
who will never leave you. He is the Holy Spirit, who leads into all
truth. The world cannot receive him, because it isn't looking for
him and doesn't recognize him. But you know him, because he
lives with you now and later will be in you.*
—John 14:16-17 (NLT)

Long ago, God spoke to a few chosen people through prophets and
miraculous signs. Now we have direct access to God through prayer
because of the Holy Spirit.

The Spirit of God lives inside each one of us who believe.

**He is with you and lives in you. You can talk to Him whenever
you want to.**

Speak to Him in prayer when you're in need. Bring Him your
questions, your suffering, your joy. God, Himself, is with you today.
He enjoys talking with you.

Try praying right now. Tap into direct access to your Heavenly Father.

Let Him know what is on your mind. He is the one with the desire
and the power to help you.

---

*Lord, You know exactly what is on my mind. You are the only one
with the answers I need. You are the only one with the power
to bring about real change. Jesus, help. Amen.*

Minister:

to give aid or service as one representing authority

You are royal priests, a holy nation, God's very own possession.
As a result, you can show others the goodness of God, for he called
you out of the darkness into his wonderful light.
—1 Peter 2:9b (NLT)

Have you ever thought of yourself as a minister or a priest?

You may be thinking, *"I love God, but I am not a leader.*
I am not an expert."

When Jesus gave His life for the sins of all mankind, He declared that
all who believe in Him are now His royal priests. What does
that mean?

It means we have the authority to show others the goodness of God.

We are living ambassadors of God, filled with His Spirit, made new
and clean, and there is no separation between us and God.

As a believer, you have full authority to stand in the presence of God,
and share the Good News of Jesus Christ with the world. Why not
do it today?

God, help me understand that I am part of the body of Christ, Your holy
church. I believe Your words…that I am called and chosen to be a living
demonstration of Your love and truth to the world. Thank You for making
me a royal priest in Your kingdom. Amen.

Indwelling:

being an inner, activating, or guiding force

**To them God has chosen to make known
among the Gentiles the glorious riches of this mystery,
which is Christ in you, the hope of glory.
—Colossians 1:27 (NIV)**

How do you connect with God?

Do you know that if you have given your life to Jesus, He is living in you right now? How can that be? It's such a mystery.

God has come to live inside each one of us who believe.

The hope of glory…Christ…living in you!

We are to be His hands and feet on the earth so that if people look at our lives, they will see a living picture of who Jesus is.

We are not in this alone and we are not relying on our own strength. God, who lives in each one of us, is here with His presence and power, guiding us, leading us, and forgiving us whenever we fall short.

---

*Jesus, thank You that your Spirit is in me. Help me shine
Your goodness, Your righteousness, Your justice, and Your Gospel
of truth out into the world. Amen.*

Conversation:
verbal exchange of sentiments, observations, or ideas

**Never stop praying. Be thankful in all circumstances,
for this is God's will for you who belong to Christ Jesus.
—1 Thessalonians 5:17-18 (NLT)**

There is no "right" way to pray.

No specific place you need to go. No special words you must say.
You can stand or kneel. You can keep your eyes open or closed.

The best time to pray is now and always.
The best place to pray is…wherever you are.
And the best posture and method of praying are…whatever you can do.

It's not so important when, where, or how you pray. It is important *that
you pray and talk to God often.*

This is how you build a friendship with God. Talk with Him in prayer
every day.

You can start with something as simple as…

---

*Lord, it's been a rough day. Would you come and comfort me?
Restore my peace in all these situations…(talk with Him about your
life and ask for what you need). Amen.*

ABOUT THE AUTHOR
Wendy Palau

Wendy Palau shoulders a burden for the brokenhearted, born out of her own experience of loneliness, pain, and loss. While raised in a loving home on the island of Jamaica, her heart sought fulfillment and peace in all the wrong places.

At 25 years of age, God radically changed her life, and she found the true joy she had been longing for. She and her husband, Andrew, have since dedicated their lives to sharing this message of hope with hurting people around the world. For the past several years, they have led multiple festivals around the United States and the world reaching millions of people and partnering with thousands of churches in cities throughout Latin America, Africa, Asia, Europe, Australia, the Caribbean, and the United States of America.

Currently, Wendy leads outreaches to women around the world in the context of Palau Festivals. She shares the hope she has found in Christ through her own personal story. She also shares the Good News through Palau's "Hope with God" Radio and digital evangelism efforts.

Her book, *Stories of Hope*, shares unique and diverse stories from multiple women from various countries, highlighting how Christ worked in their lives to bring hope in their darkest moments.

Wendy and Andrew have three children, Christopher, Jonathan, and Sadie. They live in Portland, Oregon.

*As an organization, **Palau** joyfully proclaims the Good News of Jesus worldwide because inviting people to know Him is the most loving thing we can do. Explore how God is moving through Wendy's ministry, and find out how you can partner with her at **Palau.org.***

Share Your Story

We would love to hear from you. We want to know how this book impacted you, but even more, we want to know how God spoke to you personally in your devotional times. You can send a message to ***wendy@palau.org.***